Praise for *Coming to the Edge*

Coming to the Edge

*Fifty Poems
for Writing
and Healing*

*To Andrea —
for the journey
Helen*

Helen G. Rousseau

Coming to the Edge: Fifty Poems for Writing and Healing
©2016 Helen G. Rousseau
ISBN 978-0-692-81583-0

Cover and pages design by Lindy Gifford
Illustrations by Rachel Ouelette

Rousseau Publishing
www.helenrousseau.com

This book is dedicated to
all who struggle to find their voice,
to be liberated from outside pressures to conform,
or who are healing from an abusive relationship
or one that didn't feel nurturing.

About the Title

Coming to the Edge offers two possibilities of interpretation:

At times, when we are in a difficult place, we often feel we've come to the edge of our endurance. What remains before us is the darkness of the void. We can choose to stay at that awful edge or to move on to paths that are life-giving and supportive. Many of these poems speak of being in that place. They also speak of resilience and trust that solutions will show themselves as we choose to move on.

In other circumstances, when life is going well and we've worked through our pain and struggle, we move confidently forward bathed in the light of understanding, support, love and friendship. Our hearts become full and our joy, like the waters in a rain-fed river, flows over the edge into new streams of possibility.

Contents

Acknowledgments

I want to express my gratitude to all those who have supported me on my own journey and encouraged my writing. I want to give special thanks to Susan Lebel Young, who nurtured my first attempts to find my true writing voice. To Deb Gould for our engaging dialogues and for her wholehearted support. To the memory of Robin Anasazi who had faith in me before I did. To Kerry Kenney, writing partner and friend, whose sharing over the years has kept the writing flame alive for both of us. To Rachel Ouellette, who, with encouragement and support from Kerry, provided amazing drawings for this book. To Blake Baldwin of Video Creations in Kennebunk, who encouraged me to make a professional video for my funding site. To Lindy Gifford, Brenda Tubby and Kate Albert Dawn, from my book-birthing group, who opened my eyes to possibilities and gave the encouragement to pursue them. To Debby Downs, Brad Bohon, and the York County Community Action Community who supported me in so many ways, in good times and in bad. To those in my writing groups, the birthday group, and all the friends who fill my world with joy and support, thank you.

To Susan Findlay and the late Jay Walters for providing me safe harbor. To Art Lavoie, whose friendship has saved me on more than one occasion. To Linda J. Cooke, unending gratitude.

Introduction

As a young Catholic nun, I wrote poems and songs sitting in the convent chapel. These were very God-centered, as I understood God at that time. I expressed my feelings and hopes, struggles and joys. I was living a very insular life. After leaving the convent, I attended Boston University School of Theology, where my eyes were opened to other faith traditions but still within a Christian context. I wrote many songs based on the messages of the Hebrew and Christian Scriptures. I also visited an ashram and experienced spiritual community in a whole new way. I then had to deal with questions I thought I would never have to face: What place does religion have in my life? Why are there so many spiritual traditions, and why hasn't mine brought me to an adult understanding of life and growth as a human being? Thus began a dark night of searching that seemed to go on forever. I was lost and cut off from the interior world that had sustained me for so many years.

The poems shared here were written over the past twelve years and reflect my process of searching for my own path, for clarity and to express fears and longings. As I struggled to find my true voice, writing poetry enabled me to share deep pain and doubt. I dealt with my upbringing in the Catholic Church, my frustration with trying to live an authentic life within its boundaries, and my eventual realization that the Divine cannot be defined by our human minds.

I also dealt with PTSD from childhood experiences and from too many years in an abusive relationship. Reading memoirs and self-help books and using the affirmations in Louise Hay's *Power Thought Cards* gave me the courage to draw from my inner resources, even though I thought I had none left.

I have learned, through it all, that God, however we understand that word, cannot save us from accidents or save us from ourselves or our destructive tendencies. This misconception is a fallacy that eventually causes people to lose their faith. I believe in a Divine energy that is available to all and allows us to draw strength and courage to face the challenges of our lives. We cannot be victims or passive participants. Once we awaken to the truth of our calling to be fully human, fully alive, we can set our intention to become all we are meant to be.

I have been working on this book for months, rereading and editing poems, writing introductions to each section, and in that process I went through a transformation that totally surprised me. I ask you, readers, to trust your own processes and allow new insights and challenges into your lives. As you gain clarity, may the black and white of Struggle be transformed into the colorful Dance that is your life.

How to Use This Book

I wrote *Coming to the Edge* with the intention of sharing my difficult but transformational journey. My hope is that my poems will be a springboard for your own thoughts and expression; a tool to discover your own answers, your own truth. The three sections of this book—Struggle, Transformation and Dance—are set up to use in sequence, but you should feel free to navigate to the sections and poems that call to you.

You may want to set a tone for your reading by choosing a quiet space and letting yourself settle into a reflective mood. Breathe deeply a few times and open your heart to whatever will be revealed to you, to the inner places you need to explore, to discoveries of truths that will heal, maybe challenge, and perhaps enlighten. Read the poem out loud, if you can. What is your reaction to it? Each poem has a prompt on the opposite page, which can be your starting point for writing or drawing. Some poems have more than one prompt, enabling you to use the poem more than once. If the poem or prompt doesn't speak to you, write about why. Some poems are short but the emotions run deep. There is plenty of blank space for writing on both pages. A few pages at the end of the book have been left blank for continued writing, if needed.

The suggested affirmation can be used alone or as a follow-up to the writing. It's intended to allow you to carry the theme of the poem throughout your day.

My wish for you, the reader, is that you may find clarity for your own path, deep healing, inner peace and joy as you navigate through *Coming to the Edge*.

Struggle

Struggle

This section speaks to the difficult times we all go through at various stages of our lives. There is loss, disappointment, betrayal, misunderstandings, physical illnesses, mental challenges, and a whole host of categories that can come under the title Suffering. The first noble truth taught by the Buddha is often interpreted in English as *Life is Suffering* (or stress). But that is not all it is.

The reality of life is that it is never static. We are never in a constant state of joy or sorrow, pain or good health. There is physical, emotional and spiritual suffering that can teach us lessons if we are willing to embrace them, challenge them, listen to the deeper message. Sometimes the only lesson is endurance.

Very often when we just endure and hope for things to be over, we do not face the challenges head on and later they come back into our lives as unfinished business. Working with these poems through writing can help us go deeper into our experiences and find healing, or a new ability to let go. This would be a wonderful tool to use while someone is going through therapy.

I believe in the holistic view that we do not suffer in separate parts of ourselves. In some religions, the emphasis is on this life as a valley of tears and that bliss is to be ours only after we die—if we have lived a righteous life. But life is so much more complicated than that. We are not meant to suffer now and be rewarded later. We are given one precious life which challenges us to mature emotionally and spiritually. Along the way there are struggles, joys, transformative events, disappointments, love, and the wonders of nature that lead us to awe and to feel alive as part of creation.

May working with the poems in this section be healing and help you strengthen your resolve to liberate yourself from old burdens.

1. How does the heart know it was made for more?

2. Write about a time in your life when you knew you deserved better than the circumstances you were in.

~ My heart knows and I listen.

How Does the Heart Know?

Dreams strangled
before they can form.

Words broken
over backs in the way.

Bodies hungry
with empty bowls.

Tongues tightened
with fear.

Whence rises desire,
dreams of better,

hope seeking light
in a stranger's eyes?

How does the heart know
it was made for more?

Write about a time when you felt shut down, powerless. How did that affect your life? What would you like to say to the person who acted this way? No matter how long ago this happened, write directly to that person and tell them how you felt then and now.

⌘ I am the answer I seek.

Repression

There were no tantrums
in our family home.
A father's steely gaze
all that was needed.
We didn't argue
or question his directives.
We all knew our places,
and who ran the ship.

Invisible walls
between us all;
busy minds,
but silent mouths.
I lived with questions
that had no answers,
with feelings
that found no expression.

Write about the source of your own well of sadness.

❧ I allow myself to feel, that my feelings may be transformed.

A Well of Sadness

I have been drinking
from a well of sadness
all my life.

I tried to quench
the fires of longing
from the only source
I knew: religion.

It was familiar
but not comforting,
available but not
wanted any more.

I reject it like the lover
who loved herself only,
and left me feeling
thirsty and abandoned.

What source can enfold
the child within
who still sits in her crib,
waiting for a mother's arms

but is given a bottle
propped on a towel,
left alone within the bars
that have never left her?

What were you told about yourself that affected you negatively?

❧ I am lovable.

You Are Lovable

"You are lovable"
hovers at the periphery
of her being,
seeking a way in
to some corner of belief.

Her roadblocks are quick
and ready to defend
the beliefs of a lifetime
that enabled survival.

It's not that she was told
she wasn't lovable.
She wasn't told anything
about her precious self
or possibilities.

She believed her father
who said she had
a big fanny and she couldn't
take music lessons because
she couldn't carry a tune.

She believed her mother
who said nothing.

She believed her teachers
who told her she was bad
and always disturbing.
She believed her body
with its warts and
rotten teeth.

"You are lovable"
is a refrain she is willing to hear,

hoping to learn the melody
and carry it in her heart.

Was there someone in your life who did not respect you? Write about a time when you felt belittled. Can you write to that person from a place of inner strength?

❧ I name myself. No one else can name me.

Idiot

Rolling off your tongue
with the ease
of repetition,
the sharpness
of a dagger,
it lingers in the air,
then penetrates my heart,
as if for the first time.

Battered once more,
I feel diminished.
My own breath chokes me.
I lose my balance
under the weight
of your words;
stagger away
from your wall of disdain.

1. Write about the challenges of transitioning, especially after a divorce, separation, death of a loved one, loss of a job, a friend.

2. Write about the days when you feel you can't go on.

❧ I am making my way through. I am finding my path.

Some Days

Some days I hold
my life
in my hands,
everything makes sense;
the future
bright and promising,
the past
a bitter memory.

Some days I have
every reason
to be grateful:
for friends
and a future unfolding,
a life with meaning,
the past no longer
holding power.

And

some days I just weep.

How can you "mourn what never was"? How is that a loss?

❧ I release all that never was and I give thanks for all that is.

22

Night Journey

I wake each night at three
and mourn what never was,
waiting to be free
from memories
reminding me
of how I was a fool.

I stare into the night
while others rest.
Try as I might
the fire in my breast
refuses to cool.

I feel the pain of loss
once again
begin in my heart,
as my mind travels
to the places
where I thought
I was loved.

1. What key do you need to open new doors?

2. Write about a time when you thought someone else had all the answers.

❧ I alone hold the key to my life.

Key

The key that opened the door
to my new life was poetry.
When I couldn't express my anger
toward you because it was not safe,
I had to find a passage for the words
swimming in my head.
I feared they would drown in this heart
overflowing with the tears
that had been waiting for release.

I took all the words as they came to me,
now free to write them down;
spew them out if need be,
expressing fear and anger,
loss and hope, renewal and strength.

Once the door opened, it could not be shut:
not by you, or the memory
of anything you did or said.
For now, I held the key
that opened the doors you kept closing,
when I believed you were in charge of the keys.

Why is betrayal by a representative of religion so damaging to one's soul?

❧ My soul is sacred. I am sacred.

Learning the Catechism

The parish priest came
once a week to test our
knowledge of God's commandments,

to get us ready for confession,
making sure we knew
about the wages of sin

and the straight and narrow,
like a tightrope challenge
with the devil waiting
to catch the fallen.

We were the army of Christ
on this battlefield of earth,
no end to suffering
in this "vale of tears."

No need to dream of better days
or peaceful nights.
Life's load was heavy
because a woman ate an apple.

Questions and answers
were memorized each day—
listing sins to avoid
and sacraments that saved,
making us strong
for the fight against evil.

We stood up to answer
and when my turn came,
I stared straight ahead
as he edged his hand
up my leg and loosened the garter
that held my stocking.

Write a poem or letter to an institution or person who was not honest, who tricked you, who lied to you, who made her/himself out to be someone they were not. Let it rip!

∾ I honor truth and justice.

Damn You!

Damn you, ministers of God,
blaspheming from your altars,
behind your masks of holiness.

Damn you and those who teach you
to lead your flocks in blindness,
have them drink from the well
that dries body and soul.

Damn you, leaders who stand above
and not with, separate and not equal.
Damn your rules pronounced with
the authority of the bankrupt.

You have ears that do not hear,
eyes that do not see and feet
gone astray from the path of truth.

I see you for who you are.
I condemn you to taste the bitterness
of your own words, to reap
a harvest of discontent
for feeding empty bellies with sawdust.

Your own words condemn you.
Your own behavior brings judgment.

Write about a fear that controlled you, or controls you now.

❧ I release this fear and let go of its hold on me.

Fear

Your constant
companion was fear,
kept in check
for long periods of time.

Like a creeping vine
growing out of control,
it choked your precious life,
the passion in your soul.

We watched you
captured in its spell
and could do nothing,
our voices silenced.

The fear that grew
within you could not
be healed by our love
that flowed without.

1. Write about a time when you felt alone—emotionally or physically—because there was no one to hear your pain.

2. Now write about someone who was there for you when you felt your world was falling apart: a teacher, a grandmother, a friend, etc.

❧ I connect to my higher self: the fullness of who I am.
I realize I am never alone.

Is There No One

Is there no one
who can hold me
while I cry?

Did you ever need to decide to leave a situation that didn't honor you, like a relationship, a job, or a family dynamic that wasn't healthy?

❧ I choose the paths that I will walk.

Free or Trapped

A compassionate counselor,
wise from experience,
privy to all the tricks,
asks if we want private
sessions, which I do.

"Do you feel free or trapped?"
he questions
with a steady gaze
as much as with words.

I answer to myself,
but feel it resounding
from the walls
as I try to voice
the truth I've known
for too long.

Again he asks,
and releasing my tightened breath
I reply "trapped."
The walls don't collapse
but my world slowly does.

We both know
where the path
will lead from here
but he will walk
it with me
for as long as I need.

What invisible wall still holds you back?

I choose the challenge of new.

The Mime

My hands,
flat against the invisible wall,
seek a way out
of this self-imposed prison.

The world goes on
around me, people move
and talk. I watch
but cannot comprehend.

This world scares me.
My enclosure is protection,
though closing in.

Into this self-defeating act
I introduce a blade,
cut a door, push it down,
and begin the walk to awakening.

I pause, unsure
of my destiny,
cross back
into the guarded place,
unholy though it was,
test the ground beneath
my feet, go in and out
until safe no longer feels right.

I choose the challenge of new.

What is the child within still waiting for?

ꕥ I open to the hand extended.

A Hand Reaches Out

A hand reaches out
patiently waiting
for this tender heart
to feel safe.

For the first time,
after years of waiting,
a little girl is heard,
and she grasps
the hand extended.

1. What has survival meant in your life? Write about a time when you were surviving but not living.

2. What brings you alive? How are you living now and not surviving?

~ I live in the fullness of each moment.

I've Known

I've known
for years
how to survive.

Now I want to feel
what it's like
to be alive.

What enables you to be resilient?

❧ Gently bending to change, I stay strong.

Resilience

Resilience,
my secret companion
long before I knew
its meaning,
long before
I realized
there was anything
else that could
keep me alive.

Like the reed
that bends with the wind
but doesn't break,
resilience
was my face
to the world,

protecting
my fragile self,
enabling me
to come to this point
of knowing
there is more.

Transformation

Transformation

Transformation is a process. It is not a one-time event. Sometimes we have amazing transformative moments which change our lives forever. These can be happy times, like the view from the top of a mountain, the birth of a child, or the joy of giving to someone in need. They can also be deeply painful experiences as in the death of a loved one, a terminal illness, or a betrayal by a friend. Life asks us to show up and be present, to wholeheartedly face each experience. This can change us forever. We live more deeply, we share our joy with others, or we turn our sorrow into compassion.

Transformative moments also come after hard work through therapy or spiritual guidance. It wasn't until I started to work on healing my inner child that I could finally leave so much pain behind and become more alive. Inner-child work is the key to mental health. Spiritual health and mental health are a dual process, one dependent on the other.

May working with the poems in this section bring you to a new understanding of the transformative power of facing fear, embracing hope and believing in your inner strength and goodness.

Is it possible to find healing from an injustice or disappointment yet still be able to say that what happened was not right and very hurtful?

❧ My former pain has no hold over me.

My Memory Closet

I've managed to live well,
this life without you.
Days go by—
I don't give you a thought.

Yet, hidden in my memory closet,
stuffed in the corners,
piled on the shelves,
are days of anguish
that had no end,
sleepless nights
that were a blessing
because of the quiet,
and the mantra that haunts me still:
If I could only get it right.

Some ghost dares to open
that closet door and let
memories spill out—
taking over my days,
the space I've created,
the peace I have found.

I choose to confront
those demons
that haunt me,
and with grieving
that feels endless, I let go
a little more of what never was
and never could be.

Even still, I want to
burn that closet down.

Write about an experience of meeting kindred spirits, a time when you realized you were not alone, such as when you made a new friend or found a like-minded community.

∽ I seek kindred souls to share my journey.

Longing

Deep within each earthly soul
a poignant cry begins.

Rising from unmet need,
it seeks kindred spirits.

A unified voice begins the chant
of want and need and longing.

The power of this chorus
shatters the walls

no one
thought could fall.

How can you face life with abandon? What propels you forward?

 I draw courage from within.

 I draw courage from within.

The Children and the Dogs

The children and the dogs
approach the beach
with the same abandon,

running toward the sea
in sheer delight,
ecstatic with their freedom:

chasing the gulls,
testing the waters
and daring all to follow.

The purity of their play
draws me to that place
untouched by fear.

A prayer forms within
for the courage to live my life
with the same abandon.

Write about someone who wasn't physically affectionate or verbally loving; who perhaps showed their love in what they did for you, like work in a job they hated in order to pay the bills.

❧ I express my love and gratitude to those around me.

Food for Life

Linoleum, worn between
kitchen and pantry,
witnessed the miles
my mother travelled
to feed her family.

Apron tied over her cotton dress,
she navigated the familiar terrain:
Dad in his rocker,
three children at home
who lived in separate worlds.

She was faithful at her post.
Three squares times seven
filled hungry mouths.
She was not aware
of the fast in their souls.

Love came in the apple pies,
the cookies rolled and cut
at our metal-topped table.
We enjoyed them all
but would have preferred her touch.

Write about thoughts that intrude from long-ago beliefs that you no longer believe but still have a hold on your life. Speak to those beliefs directly from your present place of knowing and strength.

❧ They are only thoughts and I can change them.

Perfection

Perfection will do you in
I read one day.
Well I'm done in,
duped again by rules
from a former
barren life.

Like spirochetes
permeating the barrier:
the shoulds and musts
come charging in
to the new territory in my soul,
where green is blossoming
in the fertile ground of trust
and promise, sown slowly
by trembling hands and
new-found strength.

I've had it with perfection
and I cast it out
into the wastelands where
it cannot thrive or grow.

1. Write about a time when you were hanging on when you should have let go. What does that tell you about fear? About wasted time?

2. Is time ever wasted when we learn from our experiences?

Surrender leads to transformation.

The Leaf

As the last flakes
of snow are falling,
a wintry blast
swirling them around,
my focus, out this kitchen
window catches sight
of a brown oak leaf clinging,
in its vulnerability,
to that naked branch
buffeted by the wind.

I see in that leaf
what I was
but no longer am,
no longer holding on
to what seemed permanent,
knowing when to let go,
knowing that surrender
leads to transformation.

1. Identify presumed obstacles in your life that were never there.

2. How can one move along on the strength of one's own breath?

3. Write a list of all the things, people, feelings, that fill you and help you to grow. Express your gratitude for each one.

❧ The energy of my life moves me in the right direction.

Coming to the Edge

The water
in my inner stream
has been rising,
filling up with grace
and friendship,
silence and peace,
compassion and joy;
gliding smoothly over
and around obstacles
that were never
really there,
moving along on the strength
of my own breath.

Now at the edge,
I spill over freely
with the power
and strength that has risen
to the surface
and must overflow.

Can you remember how it felt to be in the darkest of nights—spiritually or emotionally? Describe it, use adjectives freely.

❧ I walk toward the light—always forward.

October

In this season
of harvest,
I gather up
the fruit:
product of the seeds
planted
in that darkest
of nights
that only came
to an end
when I chose
to walk out of it.

1. If you identify with this poem, write about what has been kept below the surface that is now rising.

2. Write about a time when the dam burst and you couldn't hold in the tears any longer; when you finally told someone of your pain, allowing yourself to receive a long-awaited healing.

    I seek the ocean of mercy.

River

In the sanctuary of my soul,
from the altar of my experience,
flows a river of sadness and betrayal:
its source, the tears held in, never shed,
bubbling now like a geyser
seeking the ocean of mercy,
to be absorbed in its waters,
buoyed by its waves
and taken to a new shore.

1. You'll notice that none of the examples in the first stanza are things. They are experiences, emotions, fears or disappointments. Yet, they can have a stronger hold on us than things or people. Which line speaks to you the most and why?

2. What, from your past, do you want to leave behind? Create a ritual where you symbolically let it go. Write about what you want to carry into your future instead.

 Letting go, I find peace.

Letting Go

disconnected family
imaginary bonds
religious entrapment
vows that strangled
    all that's human
love untrue
betrayal
holding on
grasping
unforgiveness
false hope
false saviors
ego dreams
monkey mind
wounded heart

letting go, letting
go letting
go
letting

1. What fears keep you from getting closer to the flame, to an ability to surrender?

2. What is the music of your life?

❧ I dance to the music of my life.

The Flame

I dance around the flame,
so near, it singes
the hair on my arms.
I back away,
yet still I dance
in this circle,
mesmerized by the fire
and its brightness.

The flame flickers,
calls me closer,
challenges me
to surrender
and release my fear
of being consumed.

I dance
to the music of my life,
humbled and open,
one with the universal dance
of integrity and truth.

1. Read the third stanza and write what comes to mind of painful memories. Then write a love letter to yourself, using words you have been longing to hear.

2. How can you recover joy, or bring more joy into your life?

3. How is walking in hope different from wishful thinking?

～ My heart is true; it will not lead me astray.

Poem to Myself

Your spirit has been
on the back-room shelf,
hiding in safety
until this day,
praying for courage
in your struggle
to be free.

How welcome this reunion
to know you aren't lost,
but have been guided
through it all
by the truth of who you are.

As each painful memory
comes to your mind,
embrace it
and give that wounded self
the love for which you
have been longing.

As joy is recovered,
revel in it and thank it
for returning, though
slowly it may come.

As hope opens a door,
trust you will not close it
but open it more
to travel the path
becoming clear
as you walk it.

Your heart is true.
It will not lead you astray.

Write about the stone you rolled away which allowed you to walk free.

∾ Freedom comes from within.

72

Throw Cares Away

Careening down
this highway to freedom,
bitter burdens lighten,
cares are thrown away.

Saving breezes of grace
release the bindings
of love betrayed.
The detritus of my life
litters the highway.

My body revels
in this discovery of release.
No one rolled the stone away.
The choice was all my own.

No matter what age you are, write about the inner changes you have noticed in yourself from year to year.

Sixty-Seven

Sixty-seven, not slowing down.
Each challenge finds me
and I say yes.
Yes, I will go.
Yes, I will try.
Yes, I will trust.
Yes—it must be yes.

Friends, a delight
on this sacred journey
of walking into the later years,
not ready for ending
but at peace with winding down,
at peace in the joy of life shared.

Surrender comes easier
in the search for inner freedom,
acceptance, a strength buoyed up
by gratitude for being here,
now, alive, still open
to new expressions
of life emerging.

What is your good news?

I walk in peace, whole and content.

The Good News Is

The good news is:
the war is over.
Nobody won,
but I am free.

The good news is:
trust has triumphed.
Fear lost the battle
for my mind.

The good news is:
my life has meaning.
I no longer travel
through the valley of tears.

The good news is:
today is everything.
No need to remember
the anguish of yesterday.

The good news is:
I walk in peace;
body and spirit
whole and content.

1. When did you first draw outside the lines and discover there was no heavenly retribution?

2. Which boundaries have you broken or want to break?

3. Create a shape—rectangle, triangle, oblong, etc. Begin drawing or doodling within the shape and eventually go outside the borders. Open yourself to insights that may emerge.

ﮩ I am not bound by others' expectations.

Paint by Numbers

My life, for too long,
stayed within all the lines;

predictable outcomes from
borders on the page;

creativity stifled by
adherence to the rules.

Having courage to take
this blank page before me,

I begin to draw
and let colors flow,

inspiration increasing
with each new shape.

What seems blasphemy at first
becomes salvation in the end.

How can understanding impermanence help you become more accepting of change in your life?

❧ I stay in the flow.

Impermanence

Ice covers the ground.
I risk falling as I walk
to retrieve the paper,
fulfilling the rituals
of a Sunday morning.

Rain falls in torrents
as I later drink my tea,
work on the puzzles
the paper provides
for my pleasure.

Rain falls softly
as I prepare lunch,
resigned to stay home.
Suddenly the sky lightens,
full of promise.

The sun is shining
by mid-afternoon.
I dress and leave
to walk the beach
and ponder impermanence.

Dance

by:
Rachel Ouellette

Dance

"I think about the woman I have become, about the life I am now living, and about how much I always wanted to be this person and live this life, liberated from the pressures to conform. I think of everything I endured before getting here and wonder if it was *me—my wise and compassionate self*—who pulled the other younger, more confused and more struggling me forward during all those hard years. The younger me was the acorn full of potential, but it was the wiser me, the already existing oak, who was saying the whole time: Yes—Grow! Change! Evolve! Come and meet me here, where I already exist in wholeness and maturity! I need you to grow into me."

—Helen Rousseau
(from upcoming memoir)

May working with the poems in this section allow you to embrace your inner beauty, celebrate your uniqueness, and dance with a heart full of gratitude and peace.

Who, in your life, has called to your heart, and helped you find your inner beauty and goodness?

❧ I recognize my inner beauty and goodness.

86

Song of Awakening

You call my name: I know
this is what I have been waiting for—
for a lifetime; every cell alert,
on tiptoe and tense,
to hear the words of liberation,
not knowing what they could be.

You call my name: not to ask me
to do anything, not to tell me
where I am wrong, not even
to praise me.

You call my name: I awake
to truths I now can grasp,
and in that openness
a chorus follows you: parents,
grandparents, people I had forgotten,
friends and spirit guides, companions,
calling my name as a refrain.

Each cell of my body hears,
in an ecstasy of discovery:
We have heard your sadness.
You are not alone.
There is support for you now.
You deserve to have pleasure.

Strengthened by the unison
of voices in love with my being,
my own voice joins the chorus
to sing a Song of Awakening.

Write to yourself. List your talents and achievements, however small or great.

❧ I have all that I need within me.
   I accept the gift of who I am.

Become

You are a beautiful
human being.

You are a perfect flower
in the garden of your life.

You are a treasure
still to be found.

You are a poem
waiting to be read.

You are a heart
open to love.

You have all you need
within you.

Become the person
you already are.

How can you be faithful to yourself?

❧ I want to be that Alive!

After the Storm

There is no calming
of the sea
as she answers her
ancient call for tides
to follow new moon,
for wind to have its way.

She is what she is
and cannot be other.

Her calmness today
not deceitful
but equally as faithful
to her call,
her integrity whole.

This destruction,
a personal affront
to those who love her deeply,
need to live close,
build walls for safety,
as if we could own her,
or tell her what paths to follow.

She chooses her own.

I listen to her voice,
respect her power
and immerse myself in her beauty.

I hunger for this integrity.
this fidelity to self.

I want to be
that
true.

I want to be
that
Alive!

What nourishes your soul?

❧ I am one with all of creation.

Serenity

The air I take in
with each conscious breath
is better than food.
It nourishes all the places
I have opened for healing.

My breath
unites with the breathing
of the earth, its plants
and creatures.
I am one with
all of creation.

1. Where are you now on your life's journey?

2. How can sharing your journey help others to find their voice?

᪣ I'm in the world as giver.

Where I Am Now

I don't want to think anymore
about where I am from.
My focus is
where I am now
and where I am going.
Happy and peaceful,
I've arrived at the resting place
that opens me to love's embrace:
to the possibility of being
in the world as giver,
sharing my path that others
may also find theirs,
the way to their own truth
in the discovery of their voice.

What do you do to regain serenity after a hectic day?

 I create home within and around me.

A Winter Scene

I end the day here,
in centered serenity.
The full moon pierces
the sea-blue sky
overlooking snowy fields.
It calls me to leave behind
this hectic day
as a member
of the community of the highway,
where I travelled in my mind
as my car
rolled along the blacktop,
to public places and conversations,
busy times with no relief.

The moon is my witness
as home awaits me.
The landscape is calm,
not a person in sight,
no houses or traffic,
only tranquil fields—
a place of rest that gathers me in.

1. What keeps you humble?

2. Write about a time when you weren't humble and acted from ego. What happened?

❧ I am wrapped in a blanket of comfort.

Be Humble and Bold

The more I enter
the refuge
of my inner world,
the more I come to know
of love,
beauty,
and strength.

I have met myself
and found myself
wrapped in a blanket
of comfort, knowing
I am not alone.

The deeper I go,
the humbler I become,
filled with gratitude
for everything:
every breeze or bird,
every smile or word.

From this humble place
I can be bold,
can dare to speak,
call forth, encourage,
proclaim,

because I know.

Write about a place that is your sanctuary.

<svg> I am encircled by mother earth and in her arms I rest.

Sanctuary

Eternal ebbing and flowing:
the heartbeat of mother earth,
arms encircling each continent
touching sand and rock,
fertile with life:
holy place I return to
for renewal and strength.
In this ocean sanctuary
I am reborn and find myself again.

Write a fourth stanza to this poem. What new metaphor can you come up with to express your gratitude?

❧ Gratitude fills my heart.

Grateful

grateful
as the cracked-open
seed that struggles
through loosened earth
seeking the kiss
of sun

grateful
as the grown-over
shrub that submits
to spring pruning
letting in light
and air

grateful
as the wind-weary
crew that steers
into safe harbor
happy to be
home

What have you learned from nature that inspires your own life?

❧ I am one with the cycles of life.

Vespers

Who rings the bell
calling this winged community
to daily meditation?
They come from all
directions in obedient
answer to the summons;
arrive at their positions,
sit in perfect postures
facing the setting sun,
true to their natures,
inspiring fidelity to mine.

As they descend to their own
places of union with
all that is, my own body
settles itself on the sand.
I lift my face to the sun,
join the seagulls in vespers
in praise of this day
that is ending,
the grace to just be here
on this beach, knowing I am one
with the cycles of life.

What other daily rituals can become prayer?

Every moment is sacred.

A Shower

A shower
  can be a
    prayer,

a baptism
  into
    new life,

a ritual
  of
    self-love,

absolution
  and
    forgiveness.

Have you had an experience in your life that helps you understand this poem? Explain.

❦ In the silence I wait for guidance.

Only Silence

Why is not the question.
    There is no question.
There is only an answer,
    which is yes.

There is no understanding,
    only acceptance.

There is no way,
    no prayer or vow.
There is only silence.

From this silence will come
    all the answers.

1. If you do any gardening, write about your relationship to the process or what gardening does to you or for you.

2. If you are not a gardener, write about the earth and how it inspires you.

❧ The earth grounds me and is my home.

A Partnership

This plot of land calls to me:
Make me something more:
useful, beautiful, productive.
We enter a partnership
open to change, willing to struggle.
I promise my time and labor,
it promises bounty of harvest.

When all is prepared, I plant seeds,
every shape and size, holding
life and promise. Seedlings, too,
join in the effort.
Hours in the sun, love labors
with hopes of fulfillment.
I weed and water,
notice the growth and beauty,
flowers turning into fruit,
herbs perfuming the air.

I am mindful of dangers
that could take this away
so quickly: frosts that kill
or little creatures who believe
you have set the table
just for them.

A perfect match we are, as earth
yields to patience and nurture,
providing tangible
and intangible rewards.

Play a piece of music that inspires you. What images come to you? What words from the song inspire you?

🖎 I let my body dance to its own song.

112

Living-Room Ritual

Incense cleanses the room
as candle's flame rises
from this altar of sound.
There is reverence here.

Souls tell in song
of anguish and loss,
salvation, redemption,
with emotion beyond
what religion can offer.

I dance in this space,
raise my voice to life,
honor who I am:
the yin and yang
of my newfound balance.

I utter no prayers,
enter no pleas.
My body surrenders
to its joy
and freedom.

1. Choose one stanza—the one that resonates most with you—and expand on it.

2. What inner strength is needed to stand in your own space?

❧ My vision is clear.

I Name My World

It is not from the mist
that floats upon the morning air
that my hope comes.

No thief in the night
can steal my freedom.

Above and below me,
false voices beckon.
Beside me, the shrill
call to despair.

I cry out to all who can hear:
You do not shape my life,
nor do you create my path.
You have no hold on me.

All that motivates me
arises from within,
gives no credence to fear,
false promises or lies.

I name my world,
and the space around me.
I choose the seekers
who walk with me.

My vision is clear,
my breathing steady;
my purpose as solid
as the earth beneath me.

I stand in my space.

I am dancing because…

❧ I dance in freedom.

116

Dance

Dance out of your box
     and onto the sand
dance from the desert
     into the sea

dance all night long
     now, because you can
dance with the wild flowers
     that know how to be

dance for the little girl
     who watched from the wings
dance for the young nun
     with passions restrained

dance for the barren years
     when you forgot how to sing
dance in your freedom
     for all you've regained

Epilogue

I Am

I am living
fully planted
in this world.

I am nourished,
growing, thriving
through my breath.

Listening,
I move ahead
from inner guidance.

Loving,
I gather kindred
souls around me.

I am, I am, I am.

About the Author

Poetry has been the undulating flow in the inner stream of Helen's spiritual life. From an insulated Catholic Franco-American upbringing to her present Interfaith beliefs, Helen has journeyed through feelings of being alone and lost to becoming fully present in this amazing world of gifts and promises. The challenge of this journey is what Helen has always written about. As a young nun, she wrote songs in the chapel about her love for God. These became her first album, *Who Will Listen*. She later co-produced two albums of songs which interwove Scripture with experiences of social justice and the challenges of life. She also gave concerts and retreats in Massachusetts, Maine, and New York.

Helen has both Bachelor and Master's degrees in Theological Studies, completing her Master's at Boston University School of Theology. She has trained as a mediator through the University of Southern Maine. Helen is also an ordained Interfaith minister through the Chaplaincy Institute of Maine (ChIME). She is a spiritual director, having trained at the Adelynrood School of Spiritual Direction in Byfield, MA. She is available for retreats, weddings, memorial services, and one-on-one spiritual guidance.

Helen is certified in the Amherst Writers and Artists method as described in *Writing Alone and with Others* by Pat Schneider, Oxford University Press. The AWA method seeks to empower and celebrate the creative spirit in each person and change the world to one in which all voices are heard and everyone's story is valued. Helen has led many writing workshops, among which one at the Caring Unlimited Domestic Violence Program in Sanford, Maine. This two-year program produced a small anthology of prose and poetry by the participants entitled *My Truth for the World to See*. In 2008, she published her first book of poetry, *Early Childhood Education*, about growing up Catholic in the fifties. Helen is now working on her memoir. She contributes regularly to the "Reflections" column in the *Portland Press Herald*.

To contact Helen:
helen@helenrousseau.com   •   www.helenrousseau.com

40296003R00075

Made in the USA
Middletown, DE
08 February 2017